CW00406647

# WHERE THE DEAD WALK

# WHERE THE DEAD WALK

ANGELA KIRBY

*Angela Kirby*

Shoestring Press

All rights reserved. No part of this work covered by the copyright herein may be reproduced or used in any means – graphic, electronic, or mechanical, including copying, recording, taping, or information storage and retrieval systems – without written permission of the publisher.

Printed by imprintdigital
Upton Pyne, Exeter
www.digital.imprint.co.uk

Typesetting and cover design by The Book Typesetters
us@thebooktypesetters.com
07422 598 168
www.thebooktypesetters.com

Published by Shoestring Press
19 Devonshire Avenue, Beeston, Nottingham, NG9 1BS
(0115) 925 1827
www.shoestringpress.co.uk

First published 2022
© Copyright: Angela Kirby
© Cover photograph by Douglas Cape

The moral right of the author has been asserted.

ISBN 978-1-912524-99-0

# ACKNOWLEDGEMENTS

To the following publications where most of the poems or earlier versions of them first appeared:

*Agenda, Artemis, Cracking On, Domestic Cherry, Litmus, Moonstone, Morphrog, On the Buses, Perverse, Raceme, Reflected Light, Songs of the Unsung, South Bank Poetry, London Grip, The London Magazine, Ver anthology 2003, The Year 2020 Covid Poems.*

My gratitude to Ann Drysdale for her patient help and support.

Dedicated

to my children, grandchildren and great-grandchildren
with love and gratitude

# CONTENTS

# MY MOTHER PREPARES FOR THE DAY

Her morning ritual has been the same
for more than seventy years and now, blind
at ninety, she sees no reason to change –
it starts as always with an early cup of tea, then
she sits at her bow-fronted dressing-table
concentrates, sightless, on the gilt-framed
looking glass and begins to 'puts on her face'.
A little Nivea cream, light dustings from a
swansdown puff of Coty's powder in an ivory
shade, touches to the cheeks of Bourgeois'
Brunette Rose (nestling in its blue-and-gold
box, no bigger than a half-crown piece), swift
smooth strokes of Elisabeth Arden's 'Redwood'
followed by that little *mouée* she's famous for
a sort of pout, a sucking in of lips, *et voila!*
at last she is ready for whatever, good or bad
all the pills, aches, pains, falls, doctors, priests
carers and the occasional beloved visitor
that the coming day may bring her.

# SISTER NATIVIDAD TENDS OUR DYING MOTHER

She arrives by bus at ten pm, changes into white robes, 'more happy, no?' and begins to settle our mother while my sister and I sink into armchairs, watching as Sister Natty rearranges pillows smooths sheets, strokes my mother's face, her hair, all the while keeping up a non-stop murmur, '*Mira*, see how lovely you look just like Our Blessed Lady, no? *Sí, sí*, I stay with you now.'

Our mother's eyes close, she lies back, fingering her favourite ivory rosary, and at last we can relax, but too worn-out to climb the stairs, listen as Sister Natty tell us about her Order, how all are trained nurses, look after the sick and dying at home, charge just their bus fares, but now, short of novices, can only do nights.

'Sister', we ask, 'Do you nurse non-catholics?' Her face lights up '*Sí, sí*, all are children of God, no? Sometimes one will say 'Sister I don't believe in God or all that nonsense', so I tell them 'but He believes in you, waits for you with open arms', *pues*, most of them seem happier, hold my hand, *y gracias a Dios*, many die smiling'.

# YOU ASK WHERE I'M FROM

I come from a country
where the dead walk
but even here
they follow me
I feel their whispers
on my skin, at night
they crowd my dreams
sometimes we laugh
together at all those
old family jokes
but listen, now they
are calling me
calling me back to that
beloved landscape
and oh believe me
it's hard to resist.

# FATHER

Father, I am catching you up
soon I will reach the age
you were when you died
it's a strange thought, Father.

I would like to hold your hand
be caught up in your arms again
wrapped in the old safe smell
of tweed, tobacco, Knight's Castile.

Sometimes I dream of this
how it was when I was, what
no more than three or four?

Father, where are you?
Will you wait for me?
Can you forgive me?

# MISS JESSOPP'S UPRIGHT

In the drawing-room a carriage clock strikes noon
she lays aside her tapestry, goes into the hall
dons stout boots and straw hat

then walks slowly down gravelled paths
past herbaceous borders, rose garden and lily pool
nodding at favourite plants like old friends

but now she struggles to remember their names
so repeats firmly to herself 'I am Miss Euphemia
Jessopp, noted plantswoman, close friend and

colleague of the renowned collector, Mr E A Bowles'
thus reassured, she makes for her beloved herb garden
pausing to admire its formal layout, those

box-edged beds, neat rows of plants, each one labeled
and named in her elegant italic script, from time
to time she rubs a leaf between bent fingers

sighs, recalls past glories, chicken with tarragon
salmon in cream and dill or lemon thyme, new potatoes
gloriously afloat on minted seas of butter

at last she lowers her stiff body to the white bench
grateful to rest in the shade of her wide-brimmed hat
relaxes, admires the small blue flowers

on a bushy evergreen herb beside the bench, smiles
remembers – 'Indeed, yes, I *did* give a cutting
to my dear neighbour, Mr Gussie Bowles

who grew it on, nurtured it and its progeny, then named it
after me, *"Rosmarinus Miss Jessopp's Upright"*
oh, bless him, I shall not be forgotten.'

# A MERWOMAN GIVES BIRTH

Somewhere toward morning
in the small of my back
the pain uncurls a little.

Time to remember it is the sea
I come from, such moon-ruled tides
control my body now.

So there the sea-snake stirs
and the waves surge up
hover, break and sigh away.

Out of my depth, I am swept on
by a familiar flood, no turning
back, the shore far off.

A strong swell has caught me
the trick of course
is not to struggle but to float.

Sink or swim, the sea must soon
deliver a rare pearl
to this unlikely oyster.

# A DISCIPLE HAS RESERVATIONS

An etiolated Christ
is risen in gilded majesty
above the rood screen
the incense and the candles.

At the foot of the cross
a seemingly-astonished Virgin
raises a splayed white hand
to her open mouth.

Is it His sudden glory
that has surprised her
or his shame-faced followers
who are hanging back?

I could swear that one of them
is saying 'All that gold cloth!
Divine of course but isn't it
a little over the top, even for You?'

# THE HANGDOG AND THE OAK

she saw, was almost sure
the hangdog winked slyly
when he left her that morning
defiant for once, head cocked
sloping off into the foggy streets
with a suitcase full of excuses

traffic stopped, the sun screeched
to a halt, her mouth bled into a howl
the child within her died
she was hardly aware as her feet
sank through the bright rugs
and rotting boards to the earth below

where, in time, they rooted, her arms
grew wide, leaves sprouted
from her finger-tips, her hair spread
into a canopy, birds flew in
through the broken windows
ivy embraced her

moths alighted on her trunk
badgers and foxes dug their setts and earths
beneath her, squirrels built a drey
in the crook of her arm
small owls nested in the hollow
that had been her womb

but when, after years had passed
he returned and not recognising her
took shelter in her shade
she shivered, wept, sighed
and leaning down
wrapped him in her leaves

# THE AMBIGUITY OF DOORS

the door was blue, of course it was
and it was open, naturally
so through that door

or, come to think of it, a series of them
came what mattered, or what was perceived
to matter, which may be another thing entirely

for instance, behind this particular blue door
was the start of it all, the first child
and nineteen months later, the second

but between them was a packet of letters
hidden in a sock drawer
and that changed everything

the next door belonged to an idyllic cottage
yet behind it were two miscarriages,
a third child, stillborn, and three years later

a fourth, while from time to time
a few more unwelcome facts
emerged, as you'd expect

the blue door of the London house was not
left open, of course it wasn't, yet
another two children slipped in, though by then

she'd stopped counting the children, her blessings
his infidelities, in fact she no longer counted on
anything or anybody, least of all him or God

# REMEMBERING PINK TABLECLOTHS

mist has blotted out Chelsea
and the river, this frightens her
my mathematician aunt
sitting upright in the turret window
fingering her long grey hair
an elderly Rapunzel
trying to figure out just what it is
she has to remember
now that nothing quite adds up

the little carriage clock
ticks off the minutes, hours, chiming
the long divisions of her day
every ten minutes or so she asks
'Where exactly have we got to ?
I feel it's so important to keep track
don't you?' I take her out to lunch
she combs her hair, puts on two aprons
and a tennis hat, looks for a purse lost
years ago and holds my hand
for something has been subtracted
which can never be put back

the amiable Italian chatter
of the staff does not reach her
as she reads the menu to me
with a perfect accent but cannot choose
so I order food for both of us
spread butter on her rolls
pour out her wine

yet something still remains
for time and again as I remind
her to drink, to eat, she nods
strokes the tablecloth's rose folds
smiles and remembers

'when I was a girl in Derby
there were always pink tablecloths
at the Assembly Room balls, I used
to think it was so glamorous'

# ON A WET AFTERNOON IN CO CORK

It's not what we'd expected
on a wet afternoon in Midleton
County Cork but then, just
as we left the bookshop
happy to have found a copy
of Sean O'Criadain's poetry
there they were, two of them
being prodded along
by a young lad with a stick
swaying down the high street
and not that big, as elephants go
yet large enough all the same
grey, wrinkled, a little hairy
their eyes looking nowhere
except down at the road, which
made us both feel so damned
depressed there was nothing
for it but to drop in at Roisin's
for a shot of Jamesons, then
a couple or so more, plus
a plate of bacon from Gubeen
and some cheese, but even that
didn't do it and we had no heart
for the *craic,* not after seeing
them there, prodded along by
a young lad with a stick, two
small grey elephants looking
sad and cold on a wet afternoon
in Midleton, County Cork.

# BECAUSE IT WAS SEPTEMBER

I remembered you
read your name in the clouds
those large white letters

while only yesterday
your name floated in the lily pool
nuzzled by goldfish

neither seemed odd at the time
but now the clouds are grey
the water muddied

and your name has gone
from both pool and sky
God, I miss you.

# CITRIC SAPPHICS

Cleo, Cleo, see how your breasts dazzle all men
not just men but women too, me included
two dear lovely oranges, roundly perfect
oh to caress them.

Then you, Thekla, such small hands and red lips
plus your thrilling citrine scent, is it lemon
lime or orange? Zeus, must be orange!
So damn sexy, so fetching.

Clyte, how you tease me, you witch, away
I've had more than I can bear, bitch, whore
go, find someone else, another lost soul, drive
them mad, not me, damn you.

Phile, don't you hear them call, call you, all those
fragrant groves of oranges, dripping with their
fresh and tempting juices? They drive me wild, yes
Minx, just as you do.

# FOR LACK OF A BETTER WORD I CALL IT GRIEF

November, the heat stifles
St. Martin's summer
you tell me wearily, as if
I should have known.

I watch Spain's cinnamon hills
melt into violet shadows. Now
the bandages are off, only your
new and hard blue eyes are cold.

Once again I have allowed
the carrots to burn dry and though
the pan is now scraped clean
the house reeks of bitterness.

An early start on empty roads
suburbs slipping away, sickly-sweet
with almond blossom as we head
south for Sussex through beech
woods, neatly-divisive hedges
and the soft swell of the downs.

I drive, you map-read, indicating
turns with a brisk flick of confident
brown wrists at each strategic junction
while lightly discussing the best
way to ditch your last mistress.

It is painful to remember
what you said, for trying
to be honest or so you insisted
you went too far, and now
find it difficult to come back.

How careless of you, to throw
away not just my gift but it's wrapping.
I have come to terms
with the loss of my heart but
the wrapping, it was so charming
I could have used it again.

I stretch out my hand to you
across the bed but my fingers find
only the chastity of spaces, so that
I think all night how our conflicting
wills have carved this emptiness.

Such a storm, the rain threw
needles at the roof, everything
leaked, stains above us spread
and darkened till it seemed that
with a little help from you
one of the needles had
pitched into my heart.

# A LOST PROPERTY OFFICER REFLECTS

stuck here all day
I wonder about those
who've lost this stuff
and not bothered to call in

surely some military gent
will miss his medals
feel naked without them
at regimental dinners

then this wedding dress
beautiful it is, satin, lace
and pearls, found in a black sack
on the 6.45 from Hull

did she change her mind?
did he leave her at the altar?
did someone shout 'Stop!
there's an Impediment'?

how do the lame get by
deprived of crutches
the blind man tap his way
with no white stick?

but it's the parrot I feel for
Arthur, I've called him
we've struck up
this kind of friendship

'Pretty Poll, Pretty Poll'
I tease him each morning
'Fuck off', he squawks –
it cracks me up

# EMAIL TO CASS
### with apologies to Ronsard

Hey Babe, let's go check if that red rose
which like this morning flashed
her wine-splashed gear toward the sun
will, now it's dusk, seem like so hot
with colours slashed
that once were fetch as yours.

Holy shit, what just one day has done
she's like totally knackered, gone
oh Babe, too right, nature sucks
if such awesome flowers
can be like fucked
in just these twelve short hours.

Best believe me, Babe, although
like now you look well fit
salad days don't last, youth buggers off
hang in there while you can
soon you'll be like past it
as is this once fleek rose.

# 3 AM

No moon, no stars, no sirens
wail, no cat yowls, no dog howls
only a small clear voice prevails
'on whose walls will your pictures
hang, where will three thousand books
find home, who will then dust
the Staffordshire, Chelsea, Spode
Crown Derby, Famille Rose
and those Meissen figurines?'
Lying here, one thing's for sure -
when I go – which may be soon
I'll no longer know nor care.

# ALL CHANGE

Even our small back gardens look confused
seasons no longer make sense to them, roses
in particular find things difficult, decisions
no longer theirs, as twig, leaf, bud, blossom
hips all come seemingly at random throughout
the year, and not just roses, but spring bulbs
will now rise up and look around in November
shaking their heads as if to ask what the hell
is going on, while my camellias draw lots
as to which of them will open first and
when, but it's also tough for gardeners.
Should we prune, sow, feed, mulch and mow
now, or more probably, eight weeks ago?
Simpler to take it easy in shed or sunroom
merely watching as the weeds take over
thrive and die while we tell ourselves
their dead growth provides perfect habitat
for wildlife. So here we are, promoting
bio-diversity by merely doing nothing. It's
a comforting thought and there aren't many.

# A PRESENT FROM WALES

Our first holiday, we took the express to Holyhead, and then
the little train. Did I dream the woman falling through that
half-open window, her blood across the pane? 'Don't look'
my mother said, and turned my face away into her lap.

Our luggage hung above us in brown nets, above sepia
photographs of Morecambe, Rhyll, Llandudno, Colwyn Bay.
We swung along the coast on single track, the long dreamed
of sea a silver edge to our horizon, unbearably far away.

In sheltered harbourage, the evening lay calm, dinghies
and fishing boats adrift at slack tide anchorage, slap slap
among the gulls, a black line of bladderwrack strung out
along the shore marked tomorrow's limit to my bravery.

That night the dying light fell through the blue check curtains
of my room, set pinpoints of light on the wall's well charted
geography as I launched myself on a waterway of dreams
impatient for landfall on the brink of morning.

Outside the sea sucked in its breath, then sighing, breathed
again, and whispering, threw itself against the land. I dipped
my hand in clear water and woke to find the day at my feet
the sun swimming free between the white flecked shoals

of my sky high hopes and the neat starfish in mirror pools –
the week unwrapped itself before us, spilling shells, shrimps
sea-glass, a lucky dip of pebbles into our waiting pails
I have some here on my window sill, A Present from Wales.

But still in dreams I see the woman fall, and still the blood
streams down across the glass, across the rubble and my brother's
back where the long wounds crawl, along the bay, seaweed
sprawls red upon the sand. It is hard to throw souvenirs away.

# THE SUMMER OF SOUR FRUIT

From September to May happiness sang in my veins
and I sang along, 'Oh happy day, when Jesus washed my sins
away' which was seriously weird, because I'm an agnostic
while you're a practising atheist. Our house knew – ceilings
cracked, taps leaked, mice gnawed the rugs, rats died
beneath the floorboards, the bread bin we bought in France
spoke of PAIN, clouds devoured the sky, two hazels and
a bitter orange twisted with grief - I should have known.

Difficult to pinpoint exactly when that summer began
to turn sour but everything was over by June. You
visited *La Vie en Rose* and brought Julita back. I put
my foot down, said 'No way, José', booted her out. How
you sulked and snarled, then left. I tore you from my heart
but it was like jumping from a plan without a parachute
or falling through thin ice into dark waters.

All summer I shivered, the house creaked in sympathy
trees wept, ash and willow bowed their heads, shedding
green tears to the brown lawn, fruit declined to ripen.
I paced all night through our echoing house, re-read your
letters, shredded them, re-read your emails, deleted them
then emptied Trash in case I weakened and saved that one
which said you could see the soul shining in my eyes –
Dear God, how the hell did I fall for a crap line like that?

# OUR GRACIE

i.m Gracie Fields (Grace Stansfield), 1898–1979

'Out t'pop shop an'int t'co-op shop, fair clemmed'. Popping in
to see Uncle was the only choice when a family had nowt to eat –
Rochdale's finest, born over a chippie, never forgot it. Gracie
the all singing, all dancing variety Dame, pride of our alley
Royal favourite, setting off armed with Aspidistras, Ave Marias
and Thingy-Me-Bobs to entertain the boys at the front and smiling
children at the Home she set up, but always that voice, that voice.
In the end, it was 'bye-bye Archie, Monty', she chose sparky Boris
on the Isle of Capri. ' Ee, she were a grand lass, were Our Gracie.'

# IN DEFENCE OF MEN

Let us discuss masculinity, for men now complain
to me of being continually traduced. They ask
'Must we not struggle with recession, social changes
and unfamiliar mores, the admittedly overdue ascent
of women?' It can't be easy, one feels for them.

Truly, there is much about men to be loved in their
infinite variety, the long, the short and the tall, bless 'em
all, as the song goes, the fair, the dark, the russet. This
one small and wiry, that one tall, laid back; the half-pint
and the gentle giant, saint and sinner, dustman, don.

Oh, I have loved men, not wisely but far far too well –
so many things about them being irresistible, those smooth
broad shoulders get me every time as do the gold hairs
on their wrists, the long slim tibias of sportsmen and
those chunky Scottish thighs which make a kilt hang bonny.

An aristocratic nose, lopsided smile, capable hands, slim
fingers – a list which causes me to regret my retirement
from the field. But can one forget the darker side? At best
emotional retardation, casual snubs and sexism, barely
suppressed rages, at worst, flashes of violence.

Men blame such things on chromosomes and hormones
out of their control, toxic barely-understood combinations
of nature and nurture, unnatural pairings of Ys, XXs, SRY
SOX9, so occasionally, on a fine day, if feeling generous
I may, despite myself, give them the benefit of the doubt.

# STUDIES FROM LIFE

All night she howled into the wind, helpless, struggling as it screamed back at her, throwing her through a rough surf towards the rocks, swirling her down into the black sucking mouth of the Corryvreckan were she sank, again and again, until clear light, flooding from the attic window, poured over her and washed her to the lumpy shore of the brass bed.

She painted fiercely that day but nothing came together as she intended, the oils slipped, dripped or coalesced uneasily into half-formed shapes and indeterminate features until, when the light went, she sighed and wiped the brushes clean.

Outside, the November air rasped, fog twisted her one way and another, turning the gas lamps into the numinous faces of recording angels as she stumbled through the park and on through Soho, looking out for the scribbled address, her breasts sore from the fumbling wind.

She undressed quickly in the filthy room which was rank with Jeyes Fluid and something sickly which made her gag as she lay there, helpless as a gaffed fish. Behind closed lids, she tried to concentrate on last summer, on white sand and tourmaline water, on the island they'd swum to, willing her body to remember the sun's warm grip, silk-cool water, and on what had passed at the time for love. When her eyes opened, the man's masked face hung over her like a cracked moon, his stained and shaking fingers crooked as twisted thorns, were closing in for the kill. She screamed – but it was only a whispered NO and she never stopped running.

The birth was easy and her daughter proved to be placid, lying quietly for hours in an old quilt, slung high between the studio's rafters to keep her out of the way while the work and the endless bargaining went on. The child was always to remember swaying patchwork, the smell of paint and turpentine, her mother, brush in hand at the easel, strangely foreshadowed in a pool of light, and the sound of humming as something began to take shape.

# THE DOUGH ALSO RISES

I write in praise
of Omar Spunkman
who in gold letters
proclaims himself to be
the maker of cookies
and muffins and whose
white van now parked
outside my window
bears the legend
'Baking a Difference'
all day I wait for him
dream of his cookies
fantasise over his muffins
at the scent of them
and the sound of his name
truly, then, I am lost
and faint with desire
O, my beloved
admirable Omar.

# SEVENLING

(after Akhmatova)

I loved three things about him
His shoulders, his laugh
His long hot kisses.

I hated his rages, his lies
How he criticised my driving
That he always left the seat up.

Now he sleeps beneath the snow.

# A SMALL PRECIPITATION

'Bloody hell' said St Peter as he tripped over a choir
of angels, spinning them across the firmament

like flocks of small white hippos, arguing all the
way down over matters of precedence – Cherubim

before Seraphim, Powers before Dominions
etcetera, etcetera. They were still squabbling

when they hit the Himalayas and the Atlantic
dumping rain, snow and hail as they fell. 'Typical'

St. Peter thought, 'what an absolute shower –
when they get back I'll line them all up before

Himself. Ha, that'll teach them'. Down below
Mother Perpetua tells us someone must have

grieved Our Blessed Lady who has pulled her
veil across the sky, weeping, We look at each

other from the corners of our eyes as Mother says
we should own-up but none of us will admit

to those Impure Thoughts and Immodest Acts
she bangs on about, sins that shame our parents

and stain our souls. All those decades ago
but even now, dark clouds still unsettle me.

# TOE RAGS
### (a poem of many parts)

It began under the fallen arches . ''Ere'
the man said, 'I've 'ad me eyes on you'
'what cheek' said the girl, 'but Chin Chin
all the same'. That put the lid on it
soon they were bollock-naked behind
the graves, crushing the fallen hips and
haws to the joy of some giggling pupils
out on a nature walk. 'Whatcher, cock'
said the eldest. 'God, I feel a right tit'
said the man, with a prick of shame
'more of a See-You-Next-Tuesday',
said the girl, getting ahead of herself
but she couldn't face all those kids
who by now were on the last leg
back to school and keener than ever
to knuckle down to Biology homework
'No lip from you, you hormonal lot
forewarned is forearmed,' said Mr. Balls
shouldering up to the worst class of
rowdy little arseholes he'd ever taught.

# THE CROSSING KEEPER

'How are you, Tom?'
my father asked
'Fair to middling,' Tom would say

he grew sweet strawberries
beside the line, keeping the earth
at bay in sleepered terraces

each week I spent a day
with them, Tom swung me on the gate
to watch the trains go by

dug marble-sized potatoes
from the soil
found bantams' eggs for tea

leant thin and twisted
as the hawthorn tree beside the track
still in his uniform

black serge with silver buttons
Marge had sewed up one sleeve
'No need for it, Love, see?'

ten years before, the down train
took his arm, but pain still nagged it
when the wind was east

we always knew, his face
turned grey, still –
'Fair to middling', he would say

the day the telegram arrived
I'd had my egg, was waiting for the jelly
made with Carnation milk

'and a pinch of Cream of Tartar, Love'
said Marge. Tom opened it,' No answer, Lad'
he said, then turned his head

and Marge turned hers
to the photograph beside the clock
I can still hear it

hear and feel the sound, the slow
and steady beat, tick-tock, tick-tock
loud in a silent room

the following day my father called
'Sorry to hear about your son, we owe a lot
to men like him'. 'His mother frets', said Tom

forty years on when I went back
the line was closed
Tom and the gates long gone

Marge, they said, had turned a little funny
in the head, was in a Home, there were
no pennies flattened on the track

no strawberries grew in neat rows
no whistles blew, no pullets scratched
the hawthorn tree was dead.

# THE CAD

My felicitously-named
great-uncle Hampton
sowed his wild-oats wide
throughout Lancashire
and adjoining parts
of Yorkshire, causing
a statistically-significant blip
in the local population.

He died young
though presumably happy
when, returning from a tryst
his carriage overturned
and not before time
as my father said
often and sourly, he got
his hampton caught.

# THE WIDOW'S GHAZAL

Just now outside my window I heard a blackbird call
As yesterday, far away, I thought I heard you call.

A time may come when I'll no longer wish for that
Being happy enough to hear the wild waves call.

To cull my roses and the tall white lilies blooming near
Watch swallows weaving through the air, and never call

For more. Oh, not so long ago, dearheart, we'd stroll
Together, hand in hand, secure, thinking we had no call

To doubt our future, so sure love would endure. How
Could we know that soon you'd hear war's call?

You answered, took up arms, left your Angelita here
Alone and waiting till it came, that long-feared call.

# THE WISH FISH

We have scores to settle, the Wish Fish
and I, watching through the window
as the obdurate beachcomber goes

crunch crunch over the shingle
crunch crunch over the dead starfish
bladderwrack, shattered cockleshells.

He thinks we will not recognise him
that hidden beneath the wet black helmet
of his umbrella he is safe, anonymous

as if we would not know that merciless
walk, those hunched shoulders, those
hands thrust into pockets, those fingers

clenched on the polished stone of his rage
my mouth is full of his harsh aftertaste
the bitterness of ancient tea-leaves

but across the curdled bay cliffs are falling
like yellow teeth from a crumbling skull
so now I set my Wish Fish free, see him

swim through the beachcomber's dreams
replace his heart with my golden apple
the slow death of its poisoned core.

# SUMMER PUDDING

All day long we argue, and half-way through
the night, each of us quite sure that we are right.
It must be blueberries, I say, but he insists on raspberries
red currants, and some cherries, preferably black, or
maybe, at a pinch, strawberries but I won't give an inch
cooked strawberries are anathema to me and one has
to make a stand, yet he begins once more, raspberries
red currants and some cherries, preferably black.
Now as the cook, I have the edge on him, so *Never*
it must be blueberries, I say again, and that you'd
think was that, but no, not having got his way, he
sneaks out round the back and in next door to Celia
where, the bitch, she serves him *Crême brulée*.

# SUB ZERO

we heard him on the radio
this most unlikely polar hero
who'd survived against all odds
everything the weather threw
at him, and something about
his words struck both of us
we caught each other's eyes
remembering those times
when things grew perilous
the air around us turned icy
words froze in our throats
crevasses opened between us
and though most of the time
our relationship stayed just
on the right side of chilly, one
wrong word could turn things
heavy, dangerous, the weather
closing in, we'd become lost
engulfed by the resulting
whiteout and quite unable
to find our way back, either
to safety or to each other

# SHAPESHIFTER

This time you come
the size and outline
of, say, an orange
such innocence
who could fear you?
I stroke my skin
feel you tenderly
caress you, explore
your contours
your dimensions
how could it be
I never noticed
when you first
moved in, just here
down and a little
to the left of centre
yes, there, Death
my trickster friend?

# AFTERTHOUGHTS FROM ITALY

I write this from Italy, perched in an expensively converted
cowshed where in one corner stands a rough work-bench
now buffed to a rich gloss while behind my chintz-draped
Matrimoniale lies a wooden manger, also highly polished –
it would astonish the cows, don't you think? But it's useful
for my scarves, bling and slap. On other walls hang tools
and instruments suggestive of medieval torture. Such fun!

Can you believe it's ten years since my last letter, pointing
out that we could be celebrating our Golden Wedding if you
hadn't buggered off? How the years fly. Everything here
smells of rosemary, lavender and thyme plus grace notes
of sheep dung. Paradise – apart from the mosquitos which
home in like Exocets. One of the most annoying things
about you was their preference for my blood over yours.

Where was I? Ah yes. Your treachery. Though it was
exhaustively covered in my previous note, now as I watch
swallows twist between the castle's tnurrets, the Tuscan
hills fade from blue to grey, and the silver olive groves
punctuated by accusing cypresses, it occurs to me
that I forgot to ask – was it worth it? Prosecco and
prosciutto to hand, facing up to 80, plus what should
have been our 60th anniversary, there remains this faint
itch of curiosity.

But now I hear that Sandra has left *you*, only last week
apparently, pushing you out of her new Range Rover
in the middle of Clapham Common on the way back from
Waitrose, OMG, what was *that* all about? Do tell! Terribly
sorry, etc, etc but admit, it couldn't have happened to
a more deserving pair – so poor old you, alone, broke
tables turned, do you ever regret it all?

Yours, still mildly interested,

XX Francesca

PS In view of your financial situation, I enclose s.a.e
and have disguised the handwriting, my partner being
twenty years younger than you, ten inches taller, nosy –
and sadly inclined to jealousy

PPS Did you *have* to take the Hoover?

# AT HIS REQUEST

They laid him in the coffin wearing
his gardening clothes, smelling
of damp and bonfires. Stained corduroy
trousers tied at the waist with string
torn Viyella shirt, frayed tweed
jacket and that battered grey trilby
even his down-at-heel brown shoes.

Escaped from the dreary commute
of city life, content in his garden
pruning roses, clipping a low hedge
potting up spring bulbs or lavender
cuttings which seldom took, all
the while joshing with Antonio
the homesick Spanish gardener.

Uncannily like his father, a textile
magnate who loved his mills and
those who worked in them but was
never happier than in his garden
wearing the same shabby clothes
wandering from his Victorian
greenhouse to the vegetables garden
designing ever more rose beds
and filling them with Peace and
his favourite, Ena Harkness.

Though basically kind, neither could
be described as happy, we suspected
that boarding-schools or some other
childhood trauma had scarred them
so welcomed those rare times when
a sudden change of mood could
lighten everything, happiness crept in
and at last the house let out its breath.

# A GIRL CLIMBS OUT OF THE LOOKING GLASS

I watch a girl climb out of the looking glass
as she holds up the white tulle folds of her long frock
with one hand while with the other she pulls
a stole round her bare shoulders.

How young she looks, how vulnerable, that
trusting mixture of innocence and ignorance
which anyone can see is clearly destined
for disillusionment before she is much older.

Once through the gilt frame, she looks about her
seemingly bewildered, then catches sight of me
smiles hesitantly, as if perhaps she knows me
just as, more surely, I know her.

And know the shit life is about to deal her, try
to warn her, but know too that she will not listen
not believe me. Still smiling, she shakes her head
for how could someone so old know anything?

# CONVERSIONS

The sitting tenant of the ground-floor
back has been converted. All day long
she calls upon her Lord, 'Jehovah, oh
Jehovah!', the vowels awkward, eardrums
shattered by the flying bomb which
had hurled her into silence and killed
her mother in what is now our sitting
room, for the house too has been
converted, white paint and kelims
replace the embossed paper and wood-
grained lino of the past, we have erased
the dado, basil and garlic now blend
uneasily with kippers and incontinence.
'Multiple Myeloma' neighbours whisper –
the syllables roll round their mouths
and out into the street, a handful of black
marbles rattling between us, but Winnie
digs her garden, plants out potatoes
begins art-classes, samples all the local
churches.and occasionally recants, asks\
St. Anthony to find her glasses, crosses
herself, genuflects, sets flowers and candles
before a statue of Our Lady, invokes St. Jude
or the Sacred Heart, sings a fierce off-key *'Ave'*.

# SOUTHERNERS

My father thought nowt of them
Southerners, by which he meant anyone
born below a line he'd drawn
somewhere between Liverpool and Hull
by way of Walton-le-Dale.

So I knew there would be trouble
when I brought my future husband home
he was a real no-hoper, born south of
the Thames, well-spoken, double damned.

'Eh lass', said Father, slipping comfortably
into his favourite roll as stage Lancastrian
'Tha's done soom daft things in tha life
but this beats all — what a tay-pot'.

Yet when the lights went off and all the
power, it was the southerner who fixed
them. I heard my father grumble
through the froth that topped his beer
'Sithee, 'oo could tell, yon chinless
boogger's not so gormless as 'ee looks'.

I hugged him, laughed then cried. It was
the nicest thing I'd ever heard him say
high praise indeed and it was years before
I realised that he'd been right first time.

# THE REALITY OF EAGLES

nothing can prepare us for eagles
the reality of them
their indifference
the grandeur of their wings
how they subjugate the air
and the space between mountains
their shadows hovering
between us and the sun

# STONE IN LAKE ESTES, COLORADO

stone man lies still, eighteen inches from the shore
and fourteen inches below the lake's glass lid

stone man hoods his eyes and sets his mouth
stone man juts out his nose like the newly dead

stone man has lain here for a long long time
he is not about to rise up from the water

he is not about to smile, stone man looks like God
I kneel down before him, I call him Father

# PASO DOBLE

I watch a dustball spiral upward
whirling the jeep
along the mountain road
green as a grub
in a puff of cuckoo spit

nearer, the ball disintegrates
becomes grit
powdering the oleanders
and the algaroba trees
splintering the light

the jeep farts to a a stop
pupates, disgorges
two fat-bug *Guardias*
hard-eyed
under their licorice hats

a sub-machine-gun twirls
round one squat thumb
the sergeant warns us
against gypsies
and *ladrones,* smirks
asks me to go dancing

but this just slays
his side-kick
'*No gracias*' I say
'I am a grandmother'

that does it, the corporal
wets himself, the
sergeant swaggers
sweats, says '*muy bien*'
he likes an old wine best

# MA LA SPOSA, DOV'É?

It's noon in Urbino, already hot
the church we planned to visit
is closed for an expected wedding
but by now we've had a surfeit
of saints and madonnas, so settle
for macchiatos in the shade, plus
people watching. A bridal party
gathers in the square, men tanned
and scented, flash teeth and eyes
at slim girls in unfeasible shoes
improbable hats and not much in
between, girls whose breasts, to
your evident approval, float free
in half-cup bras. After some time
three blacked-out limousines roll up
decanting bridesmaids, ushers
and a posse of sharp-finned men
in mirrored shades but there's still
no bride. We fantasise – she's died
changed her mind, becomes a tart,
a feminist, a lesbian, a nun –
it's half past noon in Urbino
and still much much too hot.

# THE CIRCLE

Six wrong turns, three dead ends, clothing
snagged and torn by wire and brambles
you're growing blasphemous, but yet
although the day's a sod I won't give up.
The last farm falls away, we push past scrub
and groups of rain-drenched cattle
then suddenly it's there, the circle
seven stones haunched against the sky.
You linger by a gate, point out the dangers
how we could sprain an ankle
break a leg and not be found for hours
or even days. You're right, of course
but sweetheart, think, not so far ahead
you and I will share the safety of the grave
so while we can, let's take these shaky leaps
from clump to sinking clump of grass
and trust me, love, this one time more
for being country born, eight decades on
though stiff and not so sure of foot
I still can find a way across the bog
to reach this place that took so long to find.

# THE LANE

If it had another name we never knew it
but it took us everywhere and nowhere
turn left at the end of our winding drive
and we'd ride our horses past fields
of shorthorns, past woods where lovers
held their trysts, past the village school
where Miss Gornall held sway over
neat rows of well-drilled children
chanting long Litanies of the Saints
and Times Tables. Then we had a choice –
down the lane that ran beside the school
under the railway bridge, past the sweet shop
the presbytery, the gravedigger's house
round a corner to St Joseph's church
with its scary Pieta and Stations of the Cross
or on to the Big House with lake and gothic
folly, through the park, past the Harkin's
cottage, a right turn and down the hill
into Quakerbrook Lane. But if at the end
of our drive we'd gone the other way
the lane would take us over Black Brook
wind past Holly Bank, Woodland Grange
The Mount where Dr Bob grew his roses
and there it ended at the Main Road
from which we'd turn away, seeing always
the face of the boy who'd died there
beneath the wheels of the Preston bus.

# SPRING, 1940

'Always write in yesterday's blood.'
Bernice Rubens

Look, here I am, turning in to the long pot-holed drive, past
the five-barred gate which is never shut – and as always I pop
the blisters in its ancient blue paint – and already it's spring and
high above me the giant chestnut holds its pink candles up to
God, our mother says – and in the long woods that lie on
either side, I pick snowdrops, aconites, primrose, wood sorrel
bluebells and the daffodils which my father planted in drifts so
many years ago, long before I, an eighth and last child, was
even thought of, let alone became such a bloody nuisance, he
says, kissing me – and half way up the drive I stop at the pond
stand on the three stone slabs, throw crusts at the ducks, laugh
as they lift their fat rumps skyward – then the wood on the right
ends here at the pond and instead there are rusty park railings
running alongside our lower field with its daisies and dew pond
and now Jonathan, Lorna and my sister's Beautiful Charlotte
come racketing up to me, nuzzling the carrots in my pockets
which I share out to them, stroking their necks and their lovely
long aristocratic noses, breathing in that special scent of them –
but now the sirens sound and I'm legging it up the drive, past
the lime trees and the weeping ash while the larks, blackbirds
and thrushes are still singing – then its in at the front door
down the front hall, then the back one, then on into the kitchen
and now it's quick, quick, under the kitchen table to join all
the rest of them – and our mother is singing 'Eternal Father
strong to save, whose arm hath bound the restless wave' –
which makes us laugh, as the sea is miles and miles away.

# BY THE VLTAVA

Five o'clock, October, mist rises in the fading light
the granite setts turn like a dove's breast
to ashes-of-roses and slate blues
over-washed with mauve.

A mean-faced wind jack-boots across the bridge
hassling late tourists and the homebound
setting the painted puppets to jump and dance
at knife point.

The old man in a yamulke and a bunched-up
coat tied with string haunches down
half hidden in the shadows
of the parapet.

He plays his reed-pipe, scattering notes
into the darkening air
they float up among the gulls
that whirl out over Zofin.

The boy who slouches beside him
a question-mark against the reddening
sky, stares down at the stones
sings a harsh song.

The listeners hesitate, draw in, intent and silent
neither man nor boy acknowledge them
nor meet their eyes but a small girl
in a pink wool frock

creeps forward, squats down beside them
and puts three coins on the folded jacket
then sways to the music, rocking
from side to side

hands splayed before her face, the music feints
with her, slipping in and out of the mist
which is rising from the black-lacquer
waters of the Vltava.

As the wind retreats, the puppets dangle
and fall still, a woman pulls the child
back into the listeners, the musicians
move away

but the echoes linger for a while
then drift out across the city
and out over the tumbling graves
in the ghetto cemetery.

# PANDEMIC PLEA, PRAYER OR POLITE REQUEST

Oh may it not be yet, Lord
But when it comes, come sweet
Oh swiftly into the darkness, Lord
Let my death be fleet